Bryan Davis

Twisted Technical Studies

Odd-Meter Variations on Herbert L. Clarke's 2nd Technical Study.

For Trumpet and other Treble Clef Instruments

AF007   ©2020, Airflow Music   ISBN: 978-1-949405-02-6
All Rights Reserved. Unauthorized Reproduction is Illegal.

Table of Contents

About The Author	3
Introduction	4
Study 1A – Major	5
Study 1B – Harmonic Minor	8
Study 1C – Wholetone	11
Study 1D – Diminished	14
Study 2A – Major	17
Study 2B – Harmonic Minor	20
Study 2C – Wholetone	23
Study 2D – Diminished	26
Study 3A – Major	29
Study 3B – Harmonic Minor	32
Study 3C – Wholetone	35
Study 3D – Diminished	38
Study 4A – Major	41
Study 4B – Harmonic Minor	44
Study 4C – Wholetone	47
Study 4D – Diminished	50
Study 5A – Major	53
Study 5B – Harmonic Minor	56
Study 5C – Wholetone	59
Study 5D – Diminished	62
Study 6A – Major	65
Study 6B – Harmonic Minor	68
Study 6C – Wholetone	71
Study 6D – Diminished	74
Study 7A – Major	77
Study 7B – Harmonic Minor	80
Study 7C – Wholetone	83
Study 7D – Diminished	86
Study 8A – Major	89
Study 8B – Harmonic Minor	92
Study 8C – Wholetone	95
Study 8D – Diminished	98

About The Author

Bryan Davis is a trumpet and flügelhorn player and teacher, originally from the UK, now residing in New York City, USA. He has garnered an international reputation as a Lead Trumpeter, and is also highly regarded as a Jazz soloist.

He received his formal musical training at Leeds College of Music but considers "the road" as his true education. With over 25 years of professional experience to his credit, Bryan continues to learn from the thousands of musicians he has performed with around the world. His trumpet teachers include J. Brian Brown, Richard Iles, Gerard Presencer, Dick Hawdon, Brian Lynch and Roger Ingram.

In his early career, Bryan Davis was a longstanding member of the National Youth Jazz Orchestra of Great Britain. He also busied himself with a variety of Jazz and Commercial freelance work. Highlights included the Glenn Miller Orchestra UK, the Syd Lawrence Orchestra, the BBC Big Band, Phil Woods, Bill Watrous, Rob McConnell, Andy Prior Big Band, the Three Degrees, the Supremes, the Brasshoppers, in addition to numerous other big bands, jazz groups and production shows. In particular, the late '90s were spent with most of the greatest 'Latin' bands in the UK, as well as visiting groups from the USA and South America. These included Jesus Alemany, Cubanismo, Sierra Maestra, Isaac Delgado, Roberto Pla, Robin Jones and King Salsa, and Salsa Celtica. In addition, he played support gigs for Tito Puente and Tania Maria.

Bryan performed with a number of Theatre companies from 1999-2009, including: *42nd Street* (European Tour), *Cabaret* (European Tour), *The Official Tribute to... The Blues Brothers* (Europe & UK), *The Rat Pack - Live from Las Vegas* (West End, UK and Europe), *The Rat Pack - Live From The Sands* (US National). He is, perhaps, best known for his association with The Rat Pack, having toured regularly with them from mid 2004 to late 2009, and then occasionally up to early 2013. This was an important developmental period for him as a Lead Trumpeter.

The numerous European tours were spent largely in Germany and Austria. This led to his association with a number of groups from these countries, most notably Thomas Gansch's *Gansch & Roses*, the Lower Austrian Concert Jazz Orchestra and Otto Sauter's *Ten of the Best*, with which he still performs around the world.

In late 2009, Bryan Davis emigrated to the USA. Now a fixture on the scene in New York City, he has performed and recorded with numerous groups in the US including Arturo O'Farrill & the Afro Latin Jazz Orchestra (including on the Grammy-winning CD '*Familia*' with Chucho Valdes), the Duke Ellington Orchestra, Blood Sweat & Tears, the Vanguard Jazz Orchestra, Orrin Evans' Captain Black Big Band, the Eyal Vilner Big Band, the Birdland Big Band, the 8-Bit Big Band and Mike Longo's NY State of the Art Jazz Ensemble, among many others. US theatre credits include sub work on Broadway for *Chicago*, *On Your Feet!* and *Book of Mormon*, and the National Tour of *Legally Blonde*.

Mr Davis has also become increasingly involved with music education, not only teaching trumpet lessons, in person and online via Skype, but also leading clinics and workshops, and appearing as a guest artist, around the world; at institutions including the University of Maine, NYU and Fullerton College in California, and at festivals including the 2014 Schagerl Brass Festival (Austria), the Wartburg Festival (Germany), the Encuentro Nacional de Trompeta "Rafael Mendez" in Mexico City (2012) and Puebla, Mexico (2013). Since late 2015 he has been an adjunct faculty member at The New School for Jazz and Contemporary Music, in New York City.

airflowmusic.com

Introduction

These "Twisted Technical Studies" are a series of odd-meter variations of Herbert L. Clarke's Technical Study #2, that I originally notated for my own use, in order to challenge myself and promote mindful practicing.

After 30+ years of practicing and maintaining my Clarke Studies, I realized that it had become entirely too easy to 'zone out' while playing them and be unsure whether I'd even worked on certain keys. To get my head back in the game and keep me concentrating, I edited the 2 versions in 7/8 meter, which are Studies 1A and 5A in this collection – beamed as 4-3 and 3-4 respectively. It's remarkable how tricky it can be to play something so familiar with one note per bar missing!

To complete the set, I also notated the possible "reflections" of these patterns - playing them in reverse, as well as diatonically upside-down, both forward and reversed. With these versions in hand, I then also transposed them to the Harmonic Minor, Wholetone and "Half-Step/Whole-Step" Diminished Scales, for plenty of other opportunities to work on your keys and scale types, while tying your fingers in knots!

Throughout this book, at the beginning of each Study, you'll find instructions specific to that scale-type. Overall, there are a few things to watch out for, as you practice these exercises.

Firstly, my goal for exercises of this sort is always to play them as softly and smoothly as possible, and to maintain an even tempo throughout. Despite the brisk "target tempos" marked, it is vitally important to spend some time practicing them slowly. It is challenging to play these exercises smoothly and slowly. If you can master it, you will find it much easier to play them quickly later.

I recommend that you start out playing these exercises slurred, as marked. However, once they become familiar, you should play alternate repeats slurred and gently tongued. I prefer to begin tonguing them with a very tenuto approach, with no gaps between the notes, in order to keep the airflow smooth and uninterrupted. Once this approach is established, then you can start to play them more staccato, being careful to maintain the same sort of continuous airstream, but blocking it with the tongue a little longer between notes.

To mark the uneven subdivisions of the beat, throughout these exercises, I strongly suggest that you tap your foot on each accented note. This will help you become used to the "big beat" of 7/8 – the uneven 2 feel which becomes apparent at faster tempos.

Finally, the "target tempos" marked on these exercises are intended as a long term goal – one I'm still working towards myself. If you can develop enough facility to play them evenly, both slurred and single-tongued in the range of 240-300BPM, then you will be well prepared for most musical challenges you may face. Have fun trying – I certainly am!

Thank you for your support of Airflow Music. I'll see you on the next YouTube video. Now, go practice!

– Bryan Davis, New York City, February 2020

airflowmusic.com

Study 1A – Major

TTS-1A
Bryan Davis

The principal goal of these exercises is to play as softly, smoothly and effortlessly as possible. Mark time by tapping your foot on each accented note, and applying a breath accent.

Start out slowly and play legato. Once the pattern becomes familiar and can be executed at an even tempo, then alternate repeats slurred (legato) and gently single-tongued. A very *tenuto* tongue, with no gaps between notes, is recommended to begin with.

The marked tempo is intended as a long term goal.

©2020, Airflow Music

airflowmusic.com

TTS-1A

7

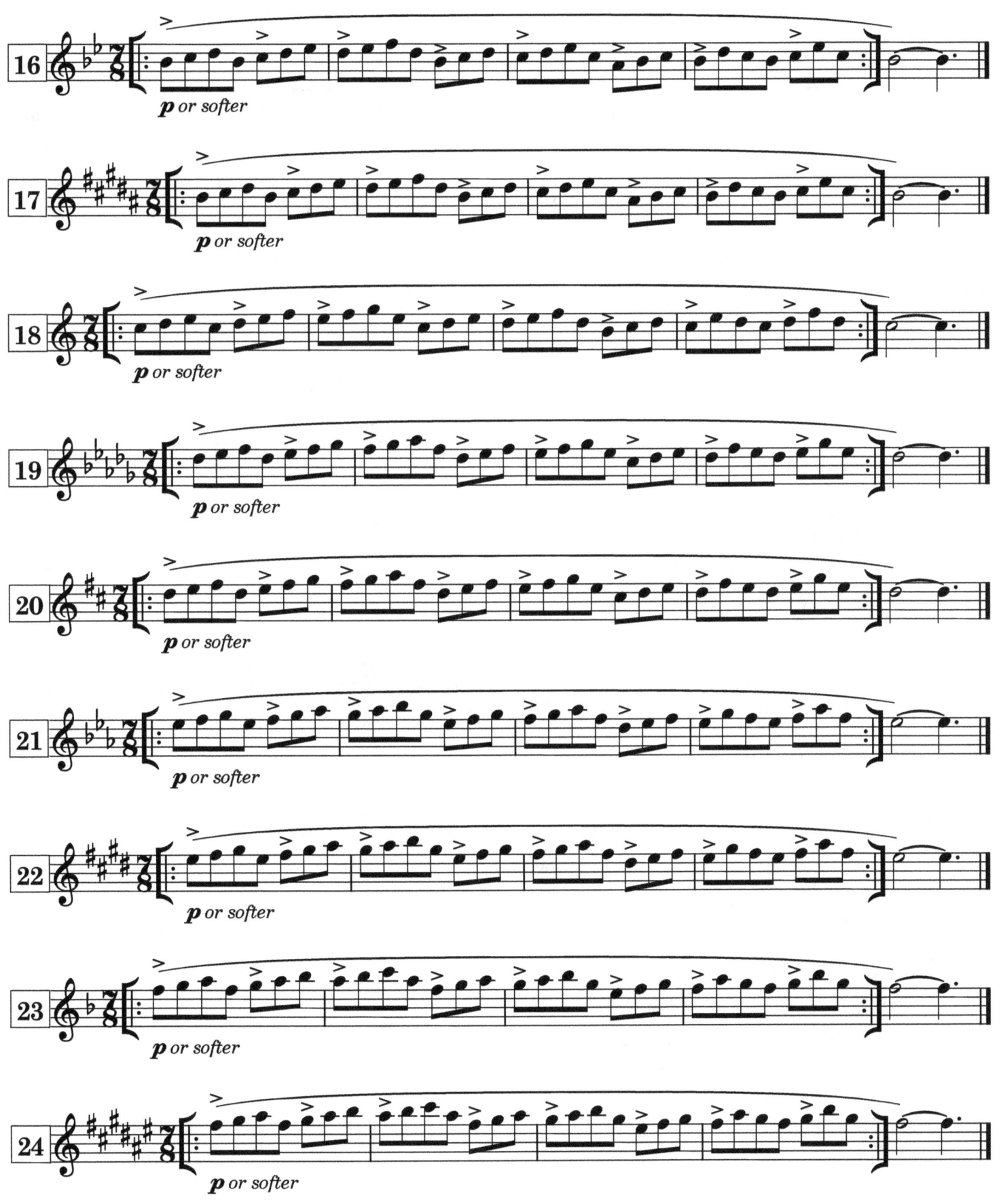

©2020, Airflow Music

airflowmusic.com

Study 1B – Harmonic Minor

TTS-1B   Bryan Davis

> We're now in minor keys, so please pay careful attention to the key signatures and accidentals during all the B sets in this book.
>
> Playing softly and smoothly remain the focus. Start out slowly and slurred, and only begin to to tongue on alternate repeats when you can play the pattern in an even tempo, without tripping over your fingers (or slide!)
>
> While working towards the target tempo, repeat each line as many times as possible in one breath.

airflowmusic.com   ©2020, Airflow Music

TTS-1B

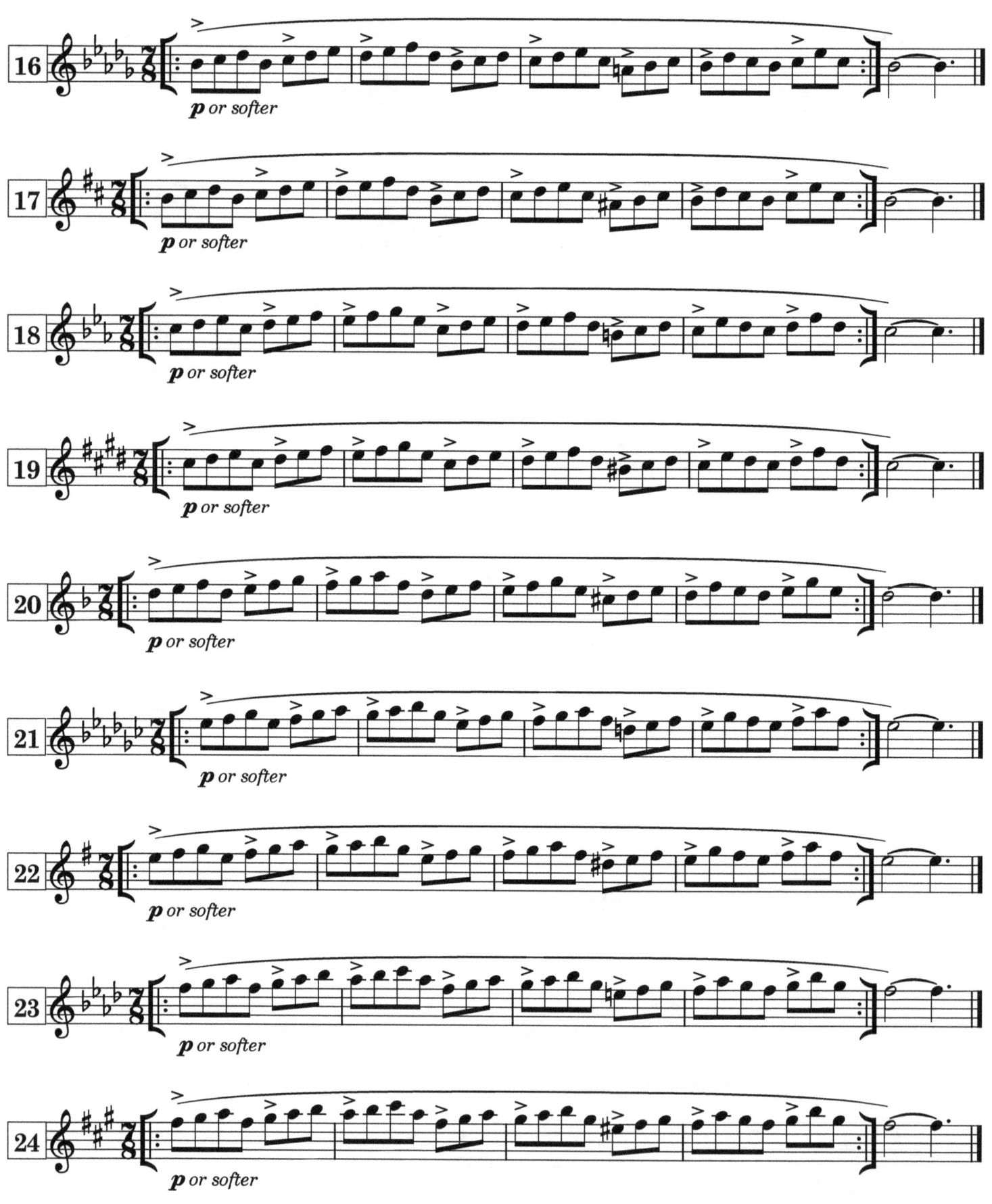

Study 1C – Wholetone

TTS-1C

Bryan Davis

All the wholetone exercises in this book are notated without key signature, so please make sure to follow the accidentals carefully.

Don't forget to tap your foot on each accented note, also marking them with a breath accent.

Playing softly and smoothly is much more important than trying to go quickly, especially to begin with. Master playing these slowly with minimum effort, first. Doing so will pay dividends later!

©2020, Airflow Music

airflowmusic.com

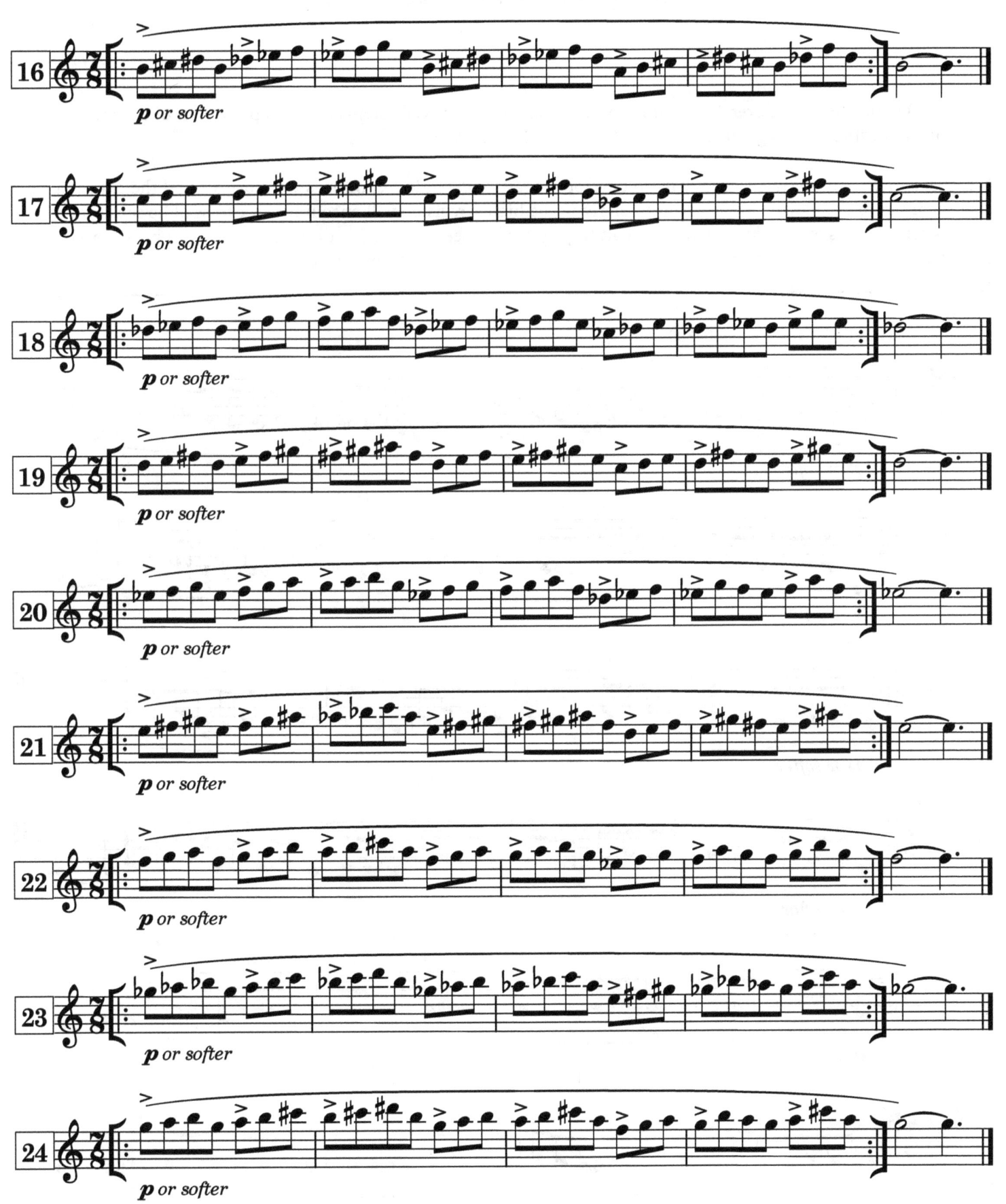

Study 1D – Diminished

TTS-1D Bryan Davis

All the Diminished scale exercises in this book are based on the "Half Step-Whole Step" version of the scale. They are notated without key signatures, so read the accidentals carefully.

Remember to play softly – we're trying to develop an easy and gentle response as we move around the entire range of the instrument. Playing too loud, particularly in the higher register, will encourage an excess of lip tension which can strain the lips and makes it more difficult to play than it needs to be. Start out as softly as can be achieved in a relaxed manner, without pinching the lips. Work to bring the volume down further over time.

airflowmusic.com ©2020, Airflow Music

TTS-1D

16

TTS-1D

airflowmusic.com

©2020, Airflow Music

Study 2A – Major

TTS-2A

Bryan Davis

Time for a change of direction! Study 2 is the diatonic reflection of Study 1, following the same patterns down the scale rather than up it. Remember that these are even 8th notes/quavers – these exercises are in 7/8 time, not 3/4 with a triplet on beat 3!

The physical approach remains the same. Take a deep breath and engage your breath support. We're aiming to play as softly and smoothly as possible. Practice slowly to begin with, slurring to keep the airflow smooth. When the sequence of notes becomes more familiar, then alternate repeats slurred and tongued.

©2020, Airflow Music

airflowmusic.com

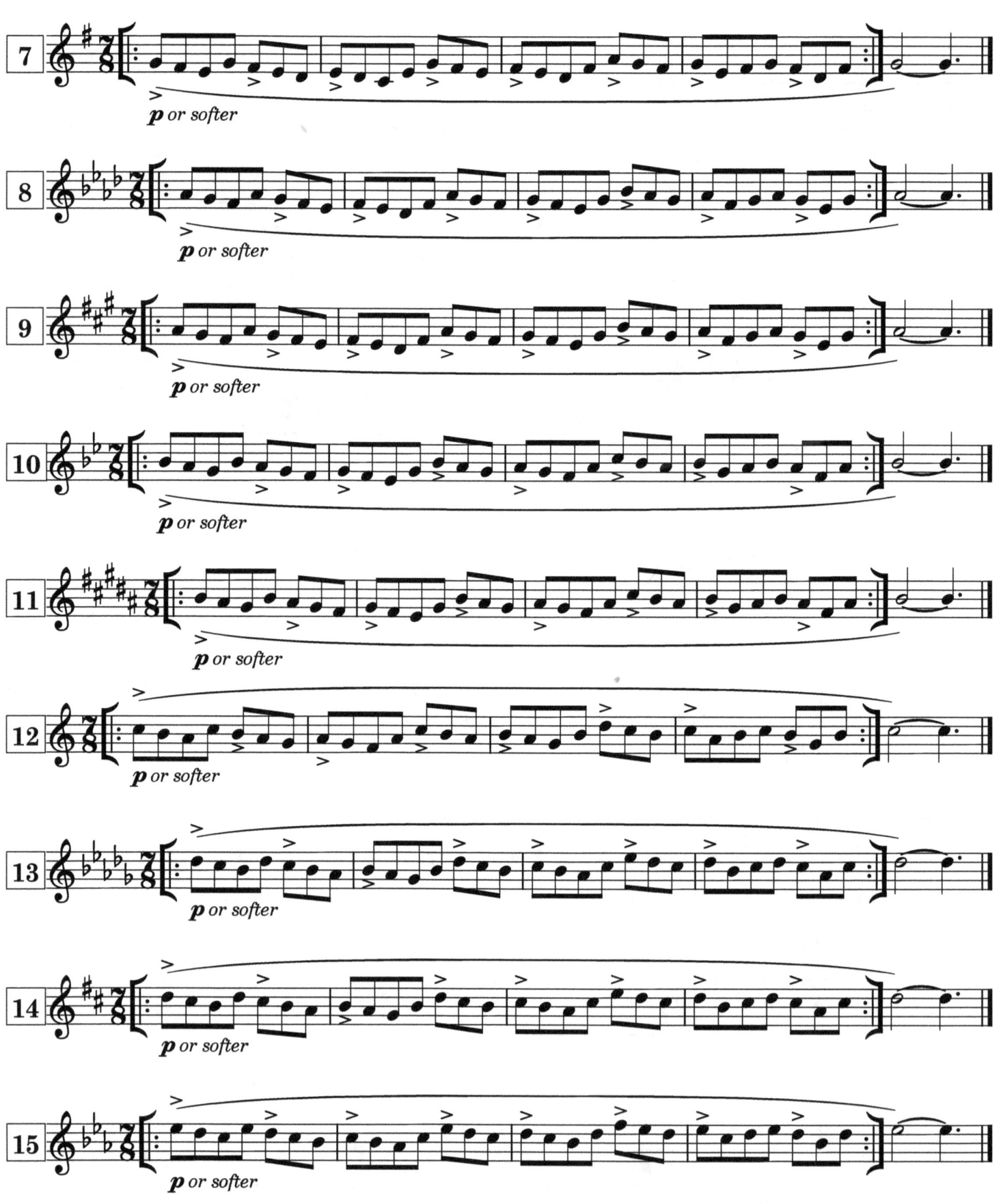

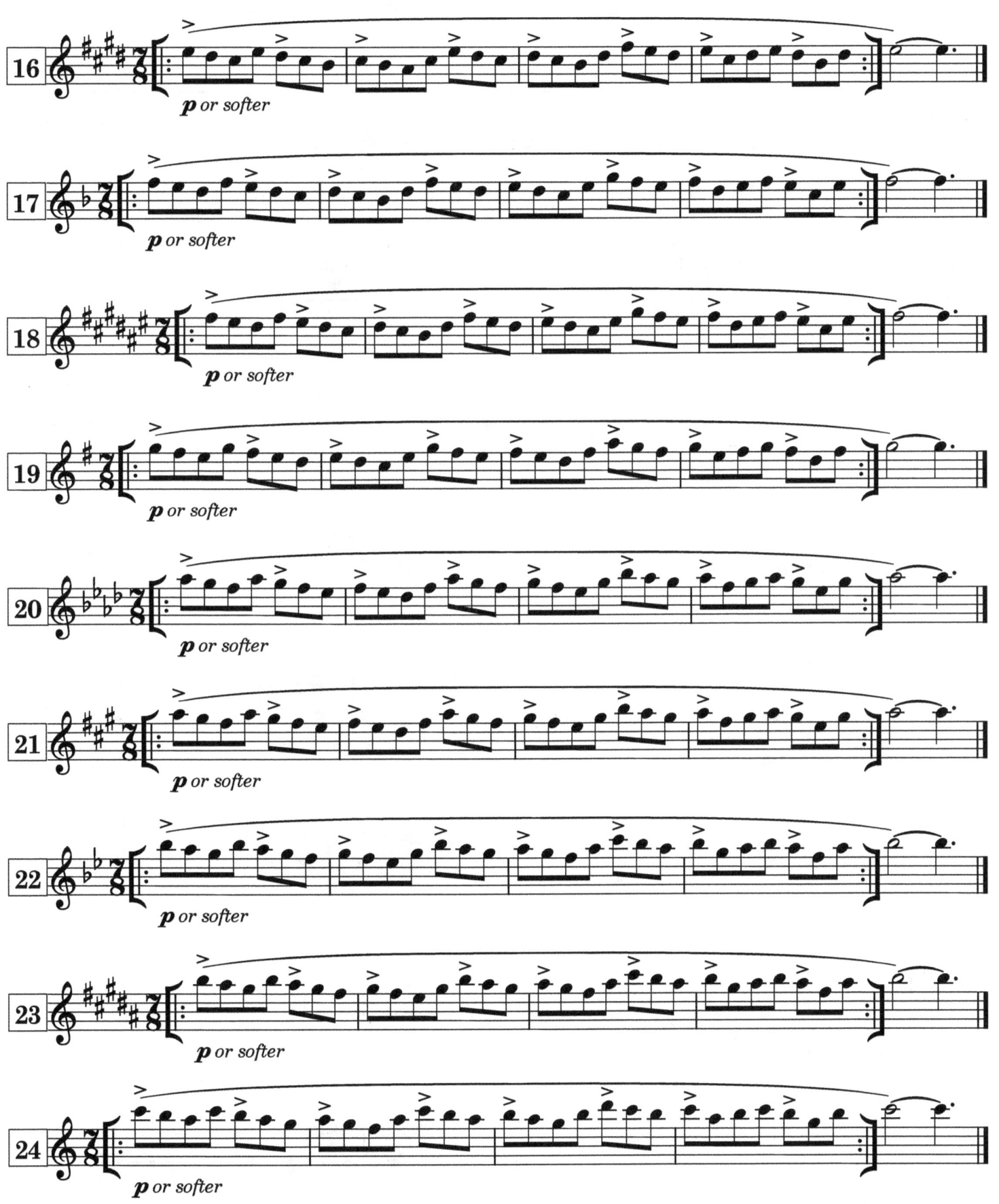

Study 2B – Harmonic Minor

TTS-2B   Bryan Davis

It is in the descending forms of these exercises that it becomes important that we're using the Harmonic Minor scale. Pay careful attention to the minor 3rd between the flattened 6th and natural 7th degrees of the scale.

While remembering to play softly and smoothly, also focus on your finger/slide technique. Try to keep your movements as fluid and precise as possible. Developing consistency and coordination in these while practicing slowly is the "secret" to building the technique necessary to play them quickly and cleanly. The target tempo is a challenging goal to achieve, particularly while single-tonguing, but it is eminently possible!

airflowmusic.com   ©2020, Airflow Music

Study 2C – Wholetone

TTS-2C

Bryan Davis

> The mixed accidentals in the Wholetone versions of these exercises hold many pitfalls for the unwary. Be sure to read them carefully, and let your ear be your guide. Mastering these exercises will improve your sight reading!
>
> The wholetone versions also contain some of the larger intervals in this book. It is especially important to practice them slowly and softly to maintain a smooth airflow through these wider intervals. Trying to play too quickly will lead to extraneous motion in your embouchure. Develop smoothness first and speed later!

©2020, Airflow Music

airflowmusic.com

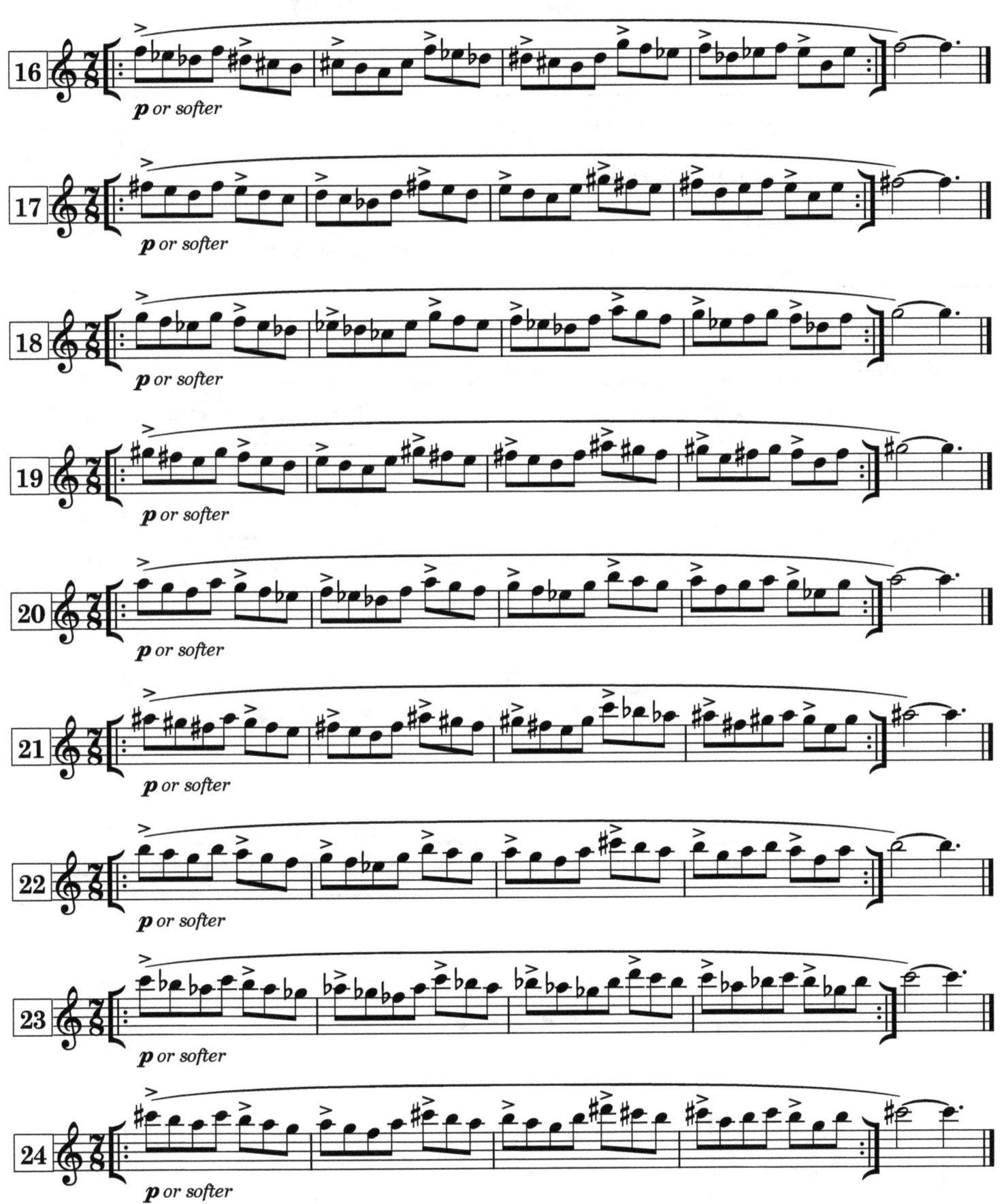

Study 2D – Diminished

TTS-2D
Bryan Davis

> The "half-step/whole-step" flavour of the diminished scale is commonly used over the dominant 7th chord in jazz improvisation. The descending versions of these exercises will familiarize you with a number of melodic fragments you may recognise from your favourite jazz solos.
>
> These are notated in open key, as before, so please read carefully. Don't forget to mark the accents by applying a breath accent and tapping your foot. Did I mention you should be practicing these softly?

airflowmusic.com

©2020, Airflow Music

TTS-2D

Study 3A – Major

TTS-3A
Bryan Davis

> Study 3 is the answer to the question "how would it go if I played Study 1 backwards?"
>
> Hopefully, the instructions for practicing these exercises are well established by now. To recap:
> Aim to play these as softly, smoothly and effortlessly as possible. Mark the accents by tapping your foot and applying a breath accent. Play slowly and slurred to begin with, to find a smooth airflow path through the exercise. When the pattern becomes more familiar, then alternate repeats slurred and tongued. Repeat as many times as possible in one breath. The "Target Tempo" is intended as a long term goal, and to be both slurred and tongued!

©2020, Airflow Music

airflowmusic.com

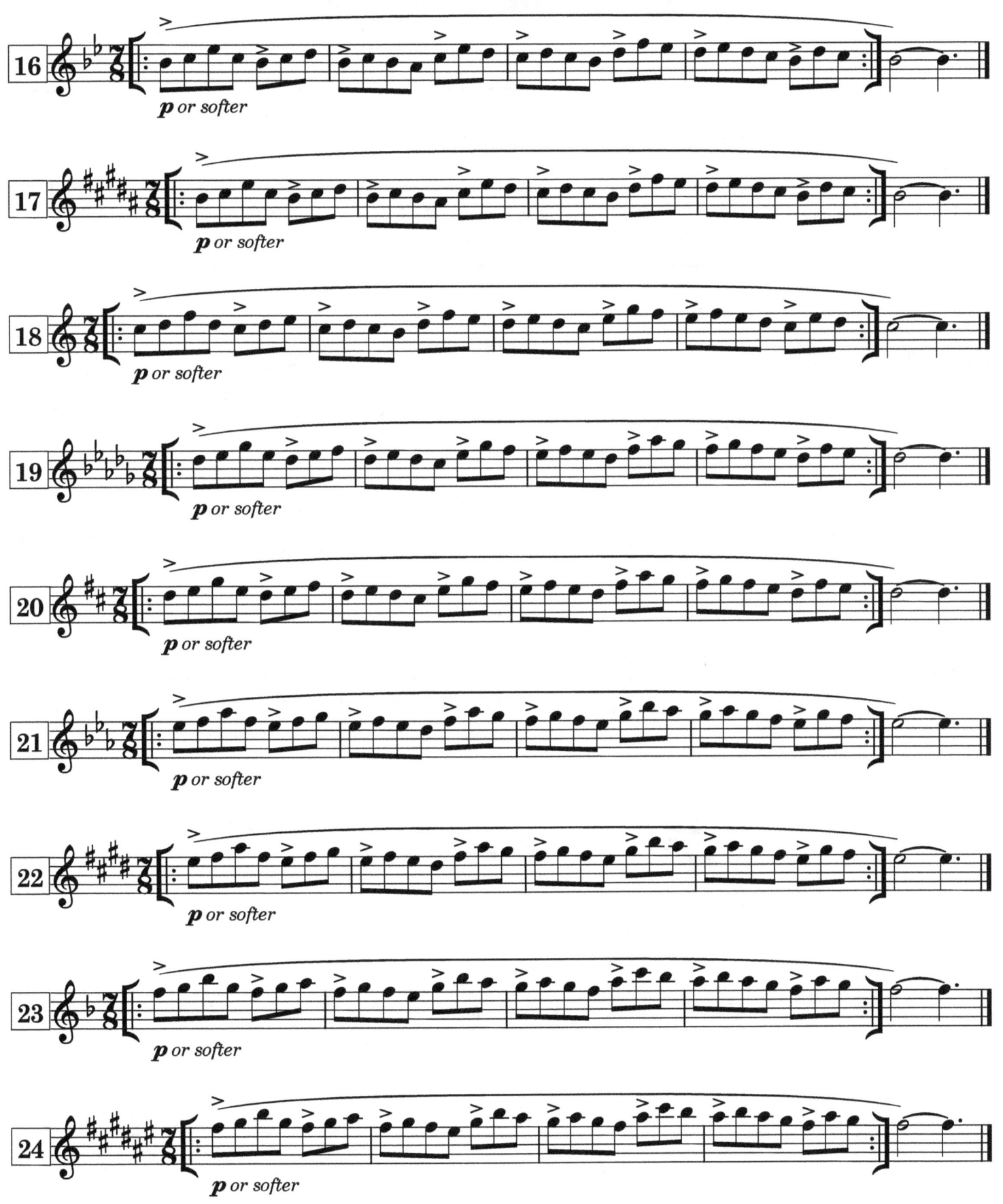

Study 3B – Harmonic Minor

TTS-3B
Bryan Davis

Remember: The principal goal of these exercises is to play as softly, smoothly and effortlessly as possible. Mark time by tapping your foot on each accented note, and applying a breath accent.

Start out slowly and play legato. Once the pattern becomes familiar and can be executed at an even tempo, then alternate repeats slurred (legato) and gently single-tongued. A very *tenuto* tongue, with no gaps between notes, is recommended to begin with. The marked tempo is intended as a long term goal.

airflowmusic.com

©2020, Airflow Music

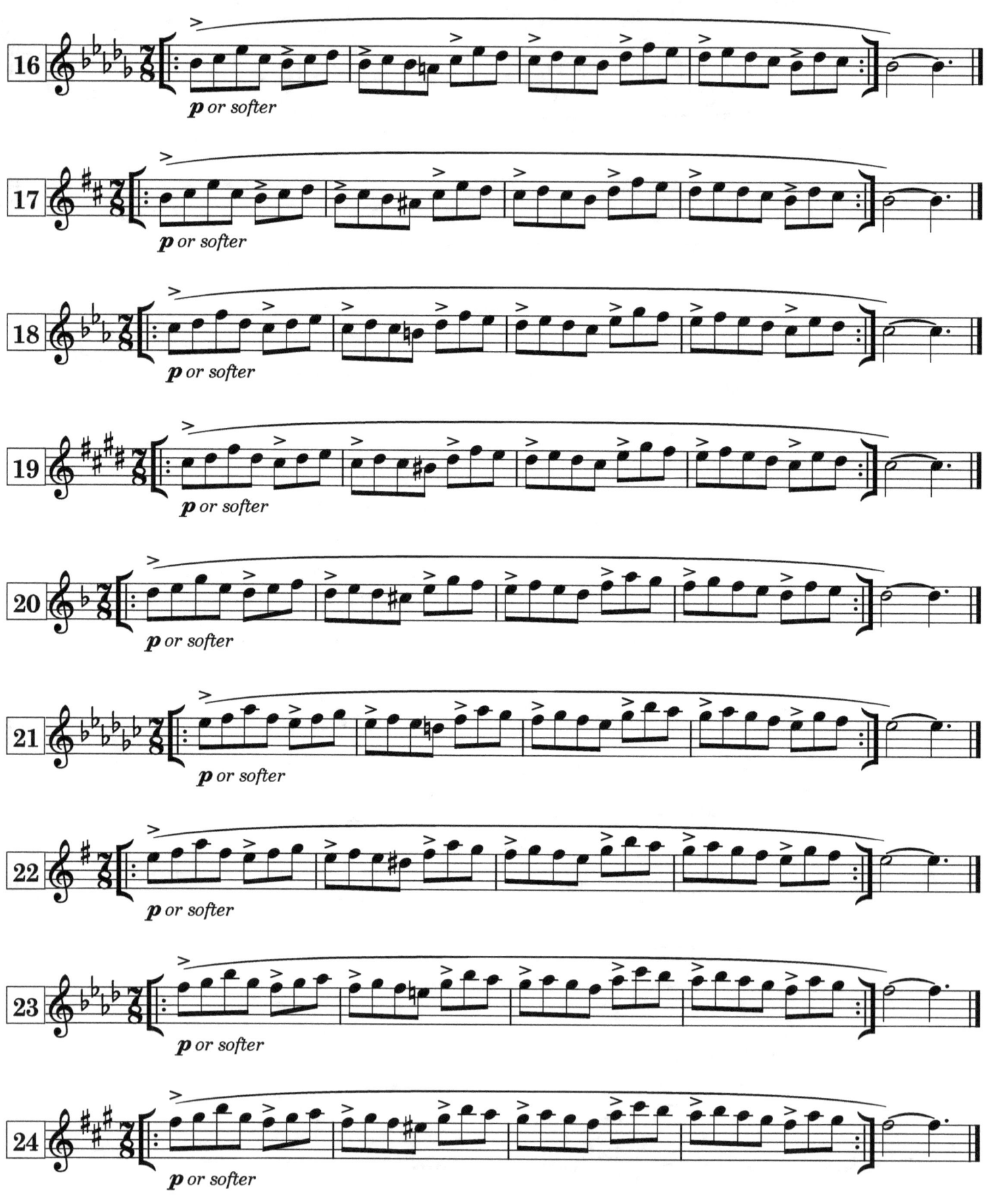

Study 3C – Wholetone

TTS-3C
Bryan Davis

All the wholetone exercises in this book are notated without key signature, so please make sure to follow the accidentals carefully.

The physical approach remains the same. Take a deep breath and engage your breath support. We're aiming to play as softly and smoothly as possible. Practice slowly to begin with, slurring to keep the airflow smooth. When the sequence of notes becomes more familiar, then alternate repeats slurred and tongued.

©2020, Airflow Music

airflowmusic.com

TTS-3C

Study 3D – Diminished

TTS-3D
Bryan Davis

> I think we all know the prescribed approach to these exercises by now. Let's face it, you've probably stopped reading these little boxes. That's presuming you're one of the few who actually reads the instructions in books like this, in the first place. If you are, you should feel quite pleased with yourself! But not too much... Read the rest then go practice.
>
> The Diminished scale exercises are notated in open key, so please read the accidentals carefully. Practice softly and slowly to begin with, focusing on trying to get from one note to the next as smoothly and beautifully as possible, whether slurring or tonguing. Don't forget to mark the accented notes by tapping your foot and applying a breath accent.

airflowmusic.com

©2020, Airflow Music

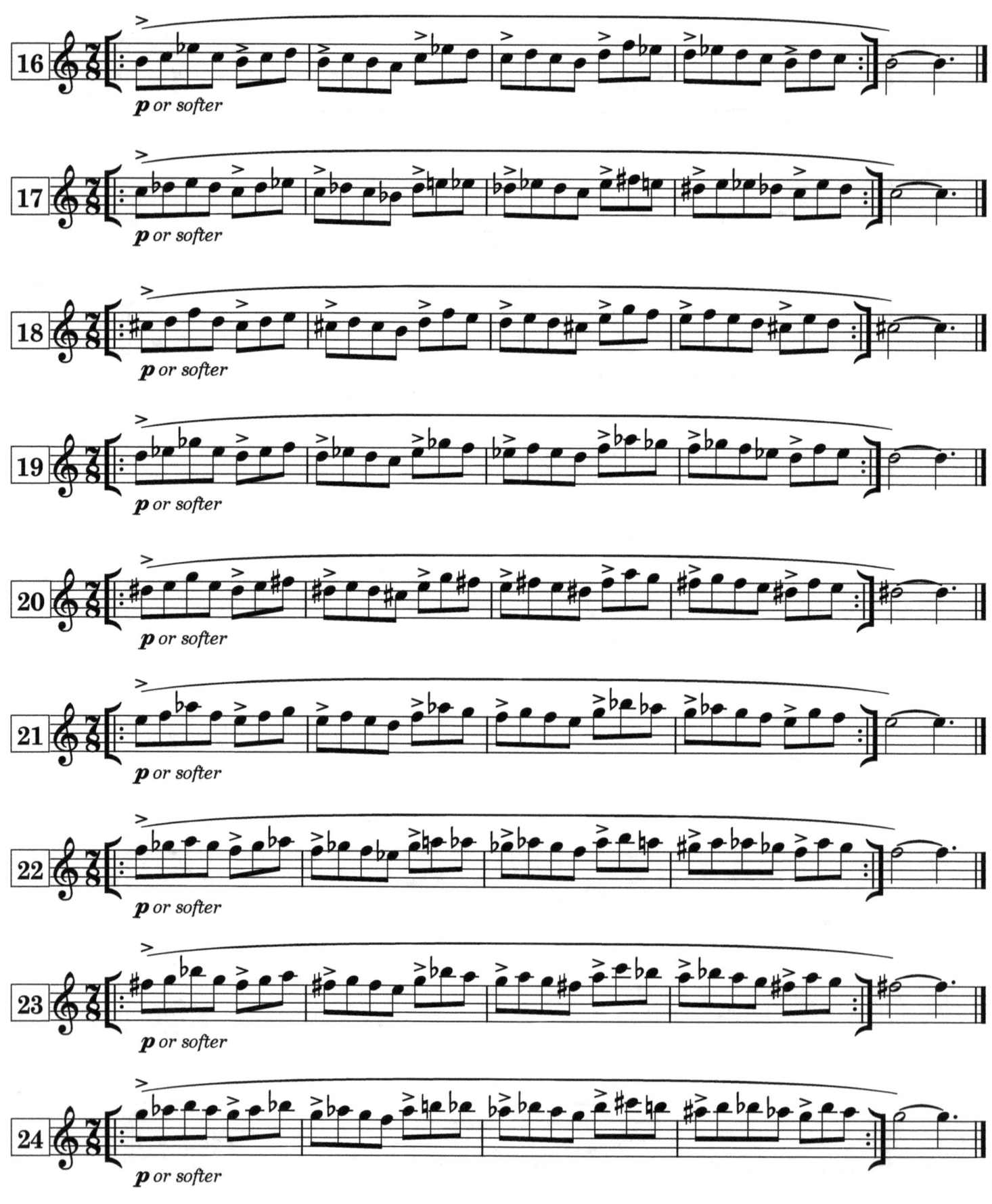

Study 4A – Major

TTS-4A

Bryan Davis

With the Study 4 set, we're completely topsy-turvy! All the Study 4s are the reverse of their respective tonalities in Study 2. Or, compared to Study 1, they're upside down and backwards!

Nevertheless, the overall approach remains the same. We are aiming to play absolutely smoothly and evenly from one note to the next, throughout each line. Go as slowly as necessary to accomplish this, to begin with. Play softly always – your starting point should be the softest you can comfortably play, while maintaining a full tone and without pinching or overtensing your lips to try and somehow stay in control of the note. Relax and let the lips respond to the smaller airstream. Gradually work towards playing softer still.

©2020, Airflow Music

airflowmusic.com

TTS-4A

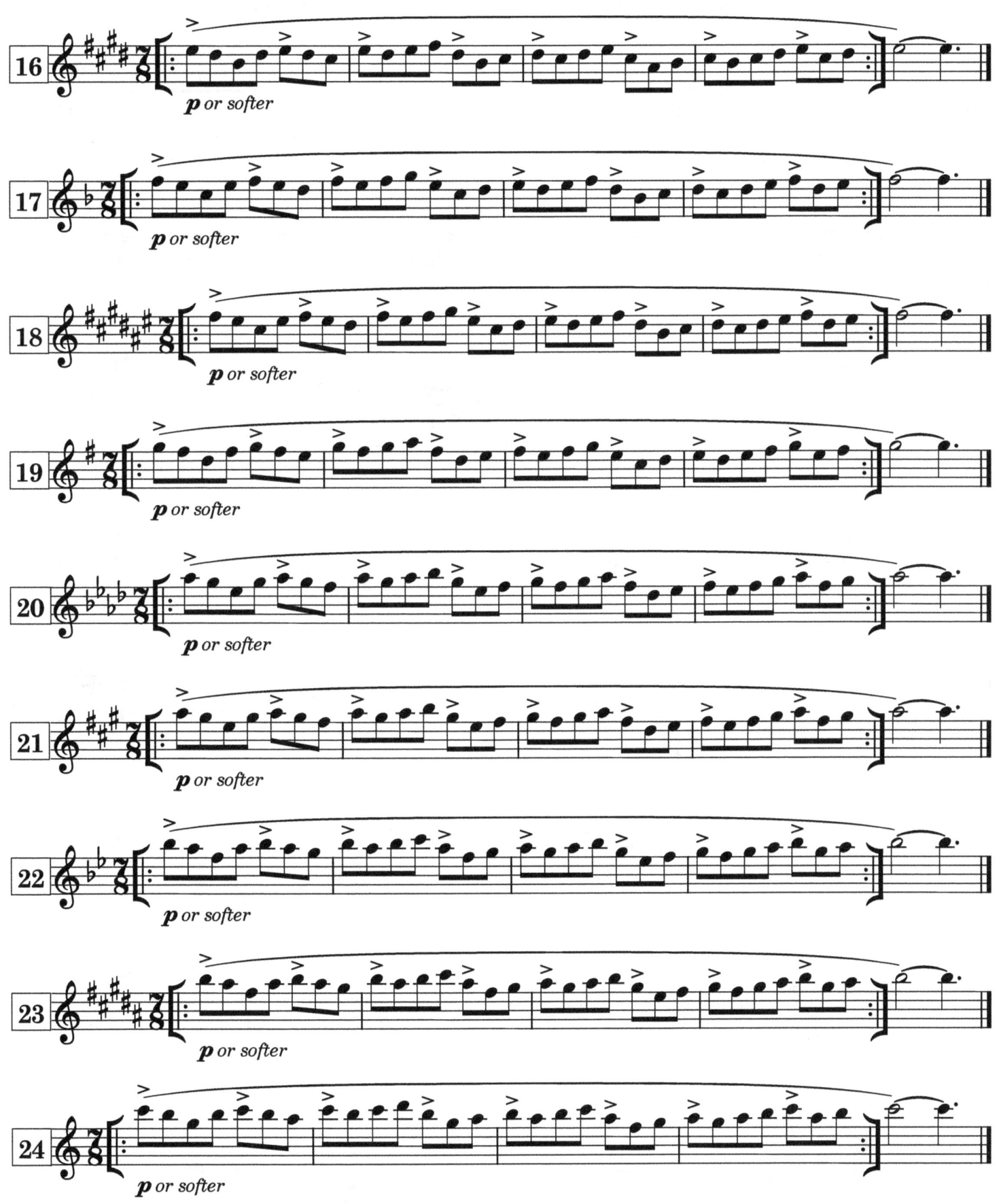

Study 4B – Harmonic Minor

TTS-4B

Bryan Davis

The Harmonic Minor versions of these Studies are my personal favourite to practice. I find that Study 4B, in particular, can tie my fingers in knots! Follow the key signature and accidentals carefully, to make sure the characteristic minor 3rd between the flattened 6th and natural 7th of the scale falls in the correct spot.

Developing sufficient facility to play these studies at the marked target tempo will be much easier if you work slowly at first, making sure to play as smoothly as possible. Being disciplined about your valve/slide technique while playing slowly is also very important – any extraneous motion is time wasted as you're trying to play faster.

airflowmusic.com

©2020, Airflow Music

TTS-4B

45

©2020, Airflow Music

airflowmusic.com

Study 4C – Wholetone

TTS-4C
Bryan Davis

> Once again, it's within the Wholetone versions of these exercises that the accidentals can get particularly confusing. Please read them carefully, and listen carefully to what you're playing, to make sure that you stay on track.
>
> Pay attention to the beaming pattern of these exercises, and be sure to tap your foot and breath accent each accented note on the page. Doing so will stand you in good stead when the beaming/accent pattern changes in another few pages time.
>
> It is impossible to overstate the importance of playing these exercises softly!

©2020, Airflow Music

airflowmusic.com

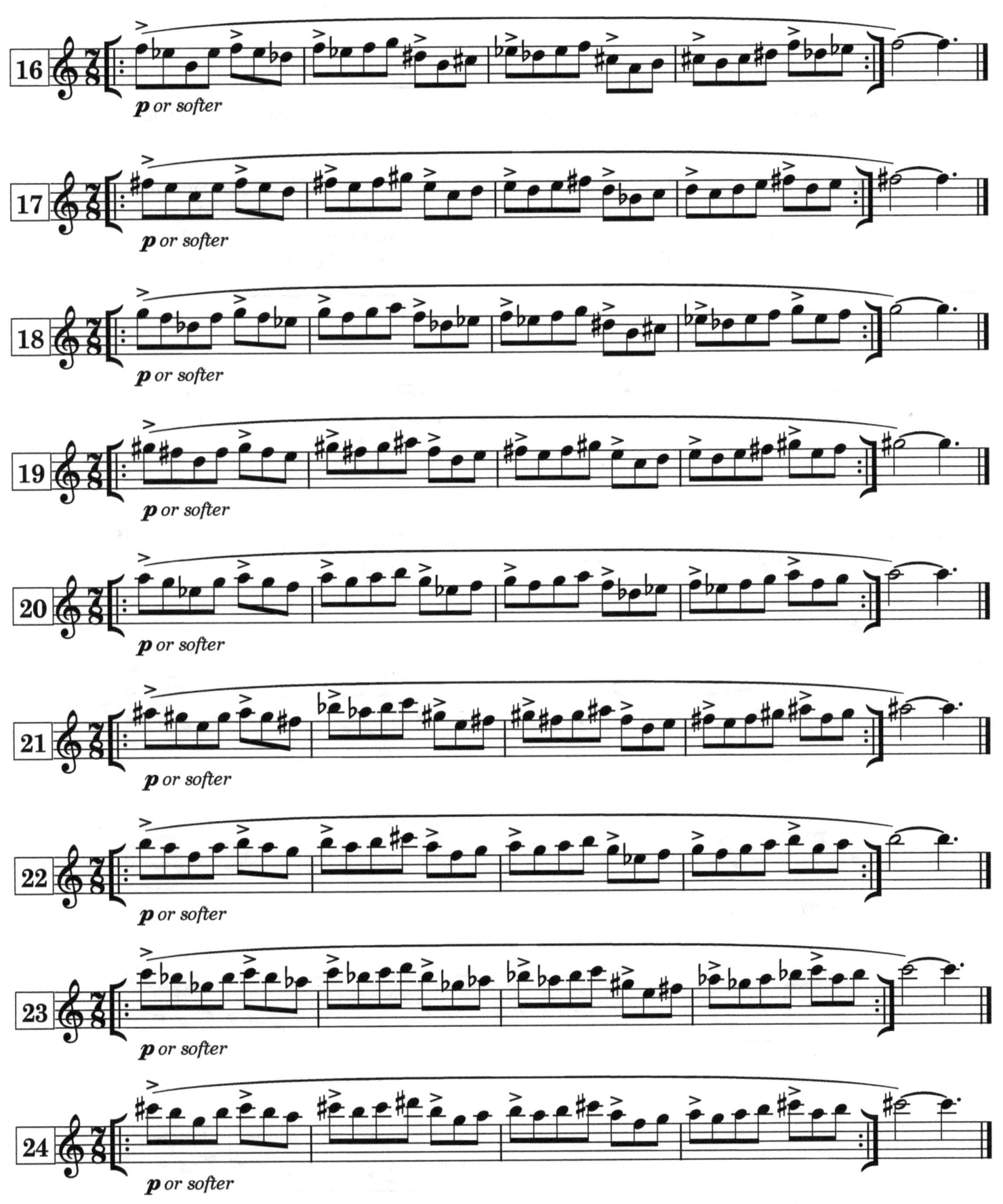

Study 4D – Diminished

TTS-4D   Bryan Davis

> *"When we perform, we're human and mistakes can happen. But when we're in the practice room, there are no excuses!"* – Sergei Nakariakov.
>
> It is important to be disciplined and intentional in how we practice our technical studies. Smoothness and even tempo, at a soft dynamic and either slurred or tongued, are very achieveable, even at the marked target tempo. We just need to start as slowly as necessary, and note any mistakes we may make so we can go back and fix them. Having patience and learning to love the process as much as the results are the keys to a happy musical life!

airflowmusic.com   ©2020, Airflow Music

TTS-4D
51

©2020, Airflow Music

airflowmusic.com

52

TTS-4D

airflowmusic.com

©2020, Airflow Music

Study 5A - Major

TTS-5A

Bryan Davis

In Studies 5 and 8, in this book, there is a particular pitfall to watch out for. Namely, be careful with the large interval drops in the 2nd and 3rd bars - in the case of the Major and Minor key versions, this is the perfect 5th between the 3rd and 4th beat of the bar. I recommend that you resist the temptation to drop your jaw when playing these larger intervals. Doing so is an unnecessary habit developed by many players, which affects ones ability to play fluidly across the entire range of the instrument. To avoid it, practice slowly through that section, and concentrate on maintaining the same level of mouthpiece pressure for both notes. The interval will most likely feel a little compressed and uncertain at first but, with repetition, the tongue arch will become accustomed to lowering sufficiently without the jaw movement.

©2020, Airflow Music

airflowmusic.com

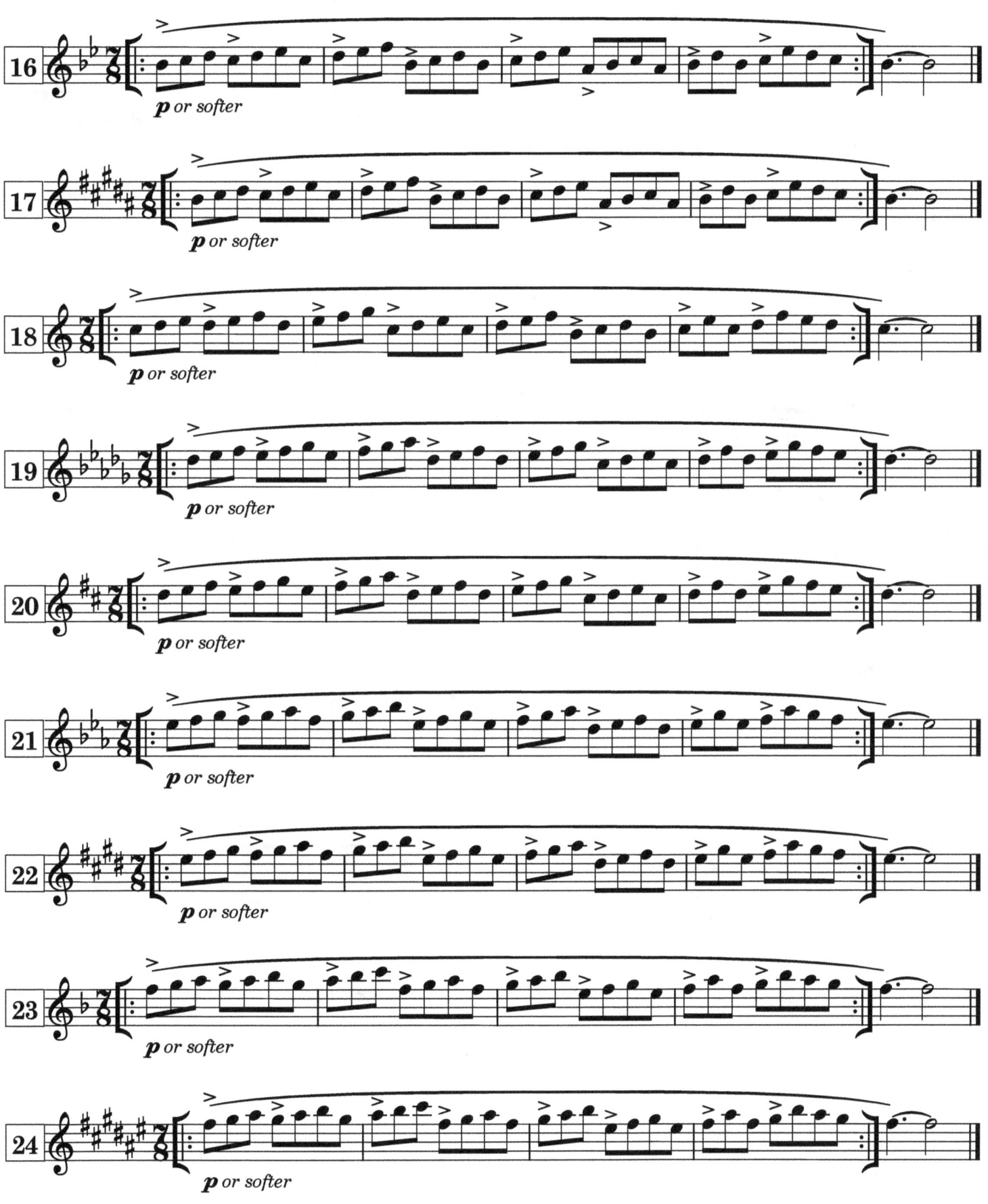

Study 5B - Harmonic Minor

TTS-5B   Bryan Davis

> We're now in minor keys, so please pay careful attention to the key signatures and accidentals during all the B sets in this book. Remember that the beaming pattern has now changed to 3-4, so mark the accents carefully.
>
> Playing softly and smoothly remain the focus. Start out slowly and slurred, and only begin to to tongue on alternate repeats when you can play the pattern in an even tempo, without tripping over your fingers (or slide!)
>
> While working towards the target tempo, repeat each line as many times as possible in one breath.

airflowmusic.com   ©2020, Airflow Music

Study 5C - Wholetone

TTS-5C

Bryan Davis

All the wholetone exercises in this book are notated without key signature, so please make sure to follow the accidentals carefully. Don't forget to tap your foot on each accented note, also marking them with a breath accent.

Playing softly and smoothly is much more important than trying to go quickly, especially to begin with. Master playing these slowly with minimum effort, first. Concentrate on your valve or slide technique, moving precisely and keeping extraneous motion to a minimum. This combination will reduce the effort required to play at faster tempi.

©2020, Airflow Music

airflowmusic.com

TTS-5C

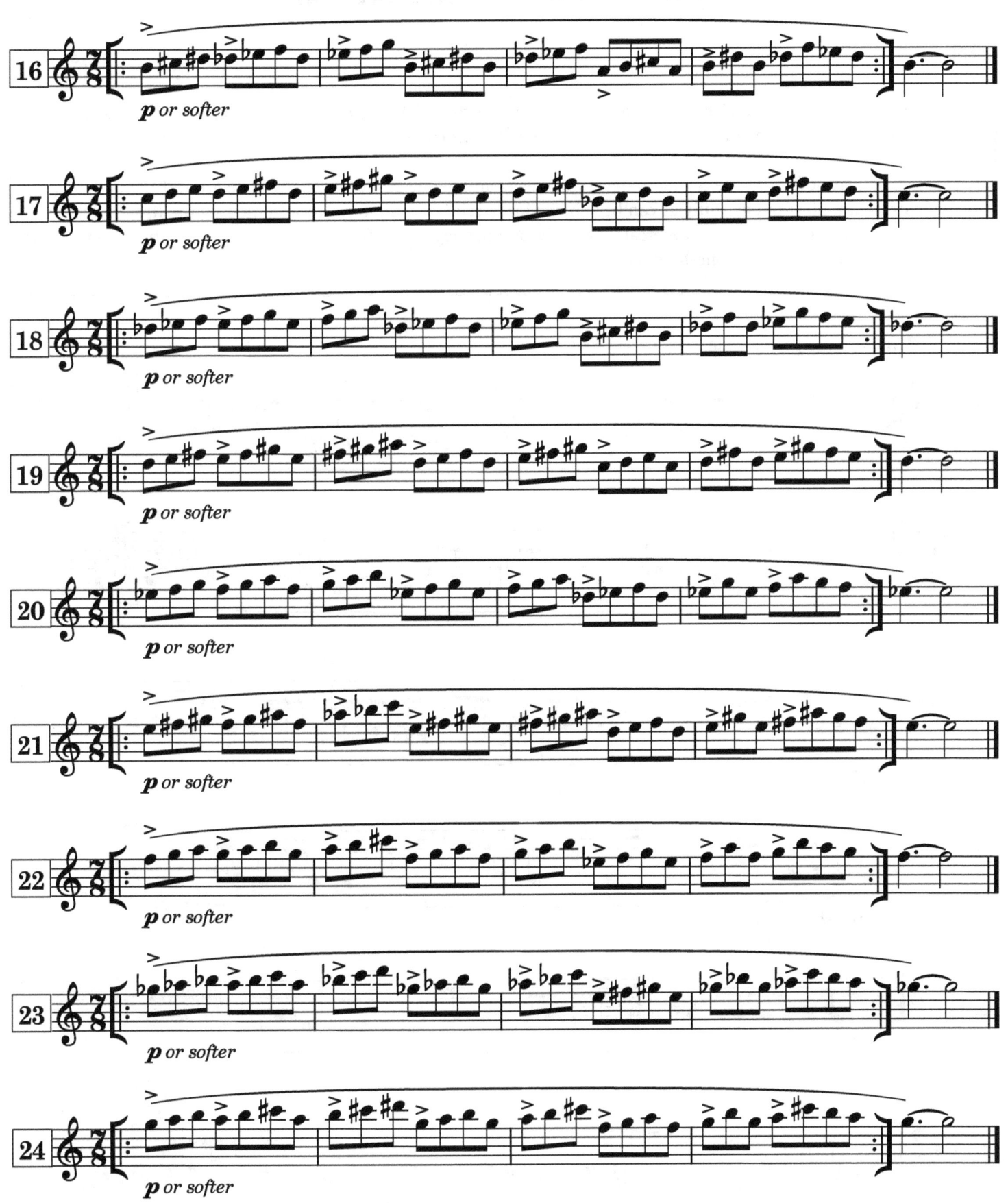

Study 5D - Diminished

TTS5D

Bryan Davis

All the Diminished scale exercises in this book are based on the "Half Step/Whole Step" version of the scale. They are notated without key signatures, so please read the accidentals carefully.

Remember to play softly – we're trying to develop an easy and gentle response as we move around the entire range of the instrument. Start out as softly as can be achieved in a relaxed manner, without pinching the lips. Repeat each line as many times as possible in one breath. Initially practice legato, to familiarise yourself with the pattern, then alternate repeats slurred and single-tongued.

airflowmusic.com

©2020, Airflow Music

64

TTS5D

airflowmusic.com

©2020, Airflow Music

Study 6A - Major

TTS-6A
Bryan Davis

Each line of these exercises should be played as many times as possible, in one breath. Don't forget to take a deep breath and engage your breath support. Remember that we are playing these studies softly, so even though we may take in a lot of air, we aren't going to be blowing hard. Instead we need to release the air without force, as we would when sighing. Try to play truly to the end of the air supply, rather than succumbing to the body's natural reflex to breathe again sooner.

©2020, Airflow Music

airflowmusic.com

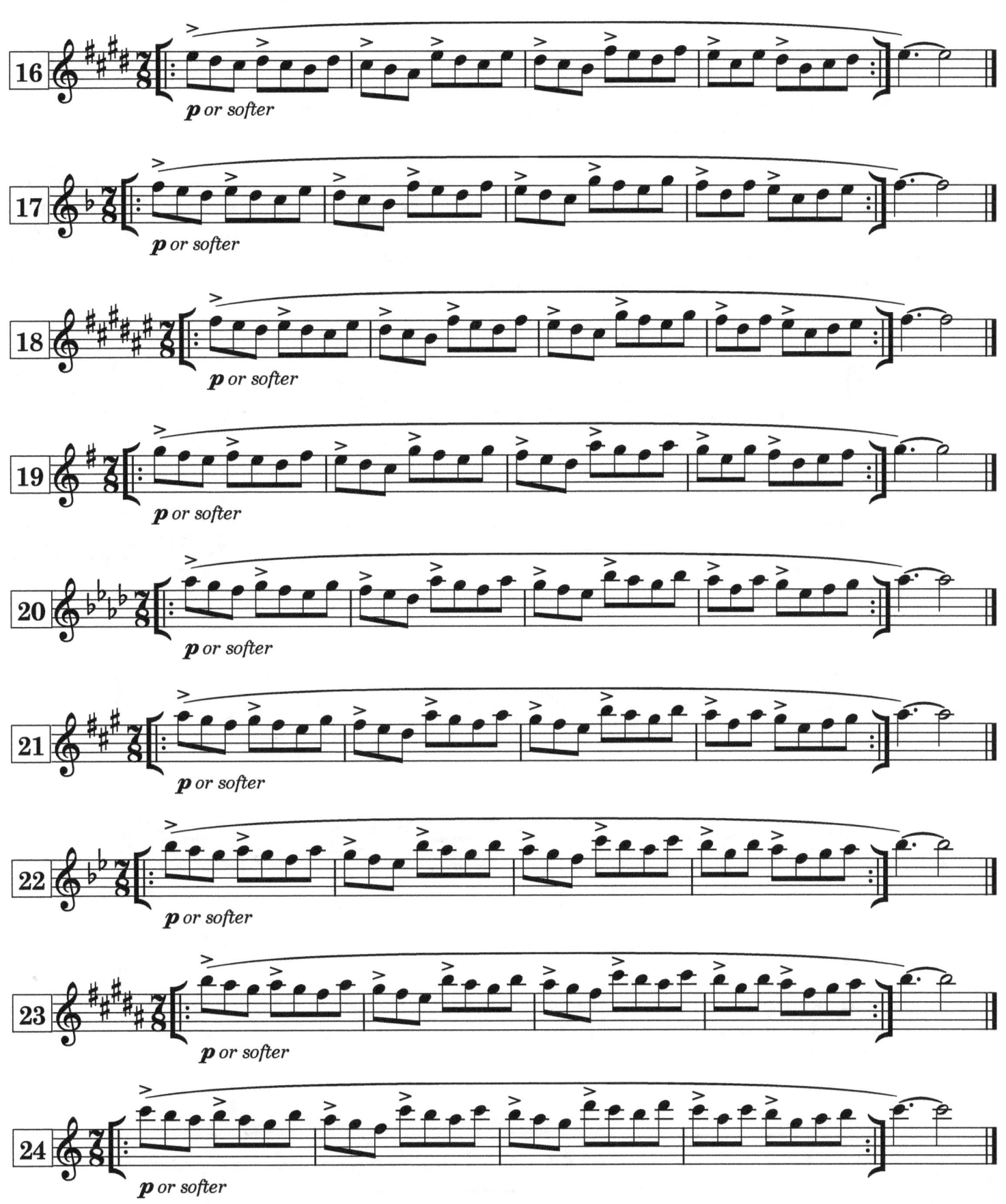

Study 6B - Harmonic Minor

TTS-6B

Bryan Davis

It is in the descending forms of these exercises that it becomes important that we're using the Harmonic Minor scale. Pay careful attention to the minor 3rd between the flattened 6th and natural 7th degrees of the scale.

While remembering to play softly and smoothly, also focus on your valve/slide technique. Try to keep your movements as fluid and precise as possible. Developing consistency and coordination in these while practicing slowly will go a long way towards building the technique necessary to play them quickly and cleanly. The target tempo is a challenging goal to achieve, particularly while single-tonguing, but it is eminently possible!

airflowmusic.com

©2020, Airflow Music

TTS-6B

69

Study 6C - Wholetone

TTS-6C

Bryan Davis

> The mixed accidentals in the Wholetone versions of these exercises hold many pitfalls for the unwary. Be sure to read them carefully, and let your ear be your guide. Mastering these exercises will improve your sight reading!
>
> The wholetone versions also contain some of the larger intervals in this book. It is especially important to practice them slowly and softly to maintain a smooth airflow through these wider intervals. Trying to play too quickly will lead to extraneous motion in your embouchure. Develop smoothness first and speed later!

©2020, Airflow Music

airflowmusic.com

Study 6D - Diminished

TTS-6D

Bryan Davis

These Diminished scale studies are notated in open key, as before, so please read carefully. Don't forget to mark the accents by applying a breath accent and tapping your foot. This is particularly important now that the beaming pattern differs from earlier exercises. Please remember to practice all of these studies softly.

airflowmusic.com

©2020, Airflow Music

TTS-6D

75

Study 7A - Major

TTS-7A
Bryan Davis

> Just as Study 3 was the reverse of Study 1, Study 7 is Study 5 played backwards.
>
> Once again, we're aiming to play these as softly, smoothly and effortlessly as possible. Mark the accents by tapping your foot and applying a breath accent. Play slowly and slurred to begin with, to find a smooth airflow path through the exercise. When the pattern becomes more familiar, then alternate repeats slurred and tongued. Repeat as many times as possible in one breath – breath support is key here. The "Target Tempo" is intended as a long term goal, and to be both slurred and tongued!

©2020, Airflow Music

airflowmusic.com

78

TTS-7A

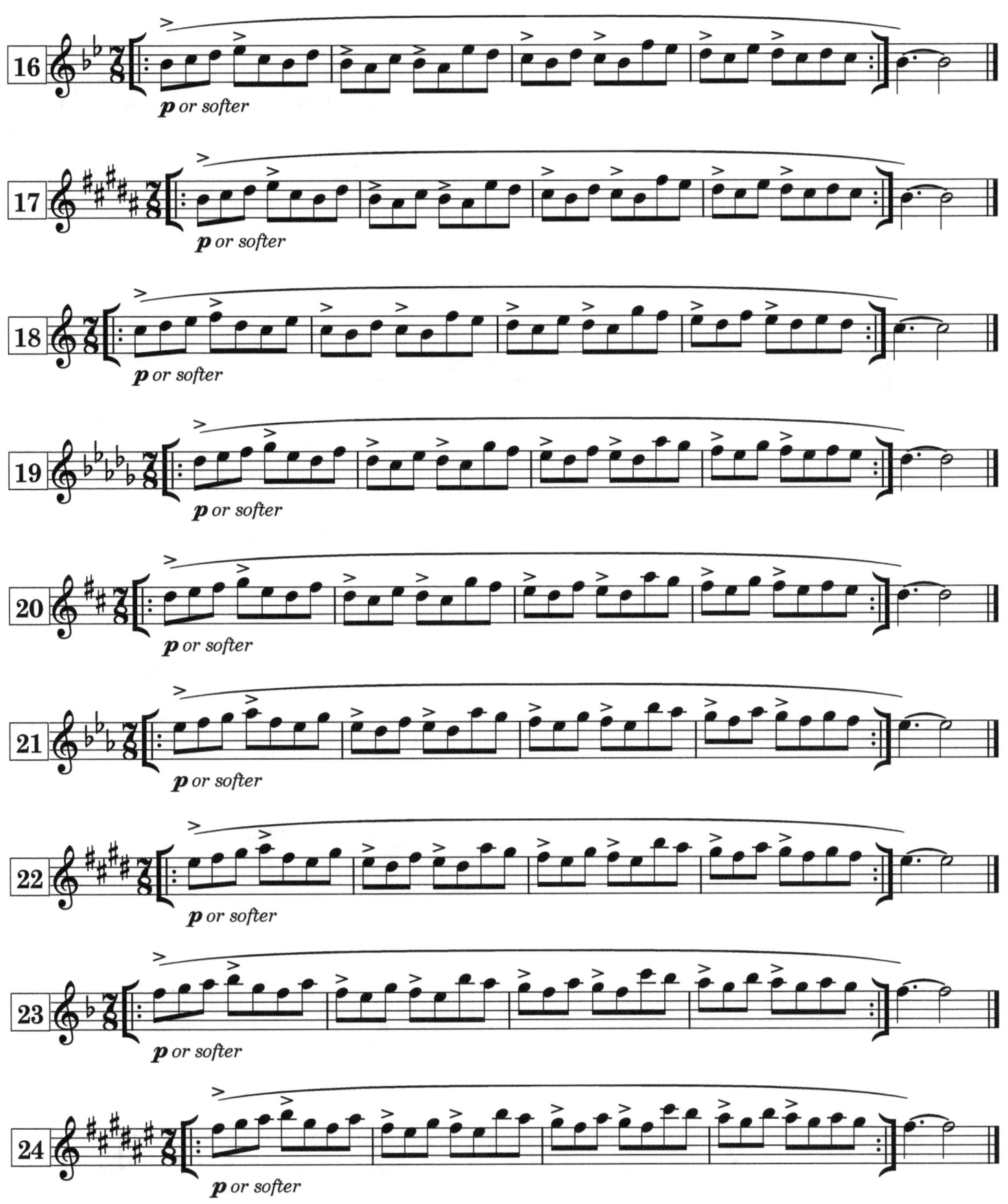

Study 7B - Harmonic Minor

TTS-7B

Bryan Davis

Don't forget: the goal of these exercises is to play as softly, smoothly and effortlessly as possible. Mark time by tapping your foot on each accented note, and applying a breath accent.

Start out slowly and play legato. Once the pattern becomes familiar and can be executed at an even tempo, then alternate repeats slurred (legato) and gently single-tongued. A very *tenuto* tongue, with no gaps between notes, is recommended to begin with. Remember to take a deep breath, engage your breath support and play each line as many times as possible in one breath.

airflowmusic.com

©2020, Airflow Music

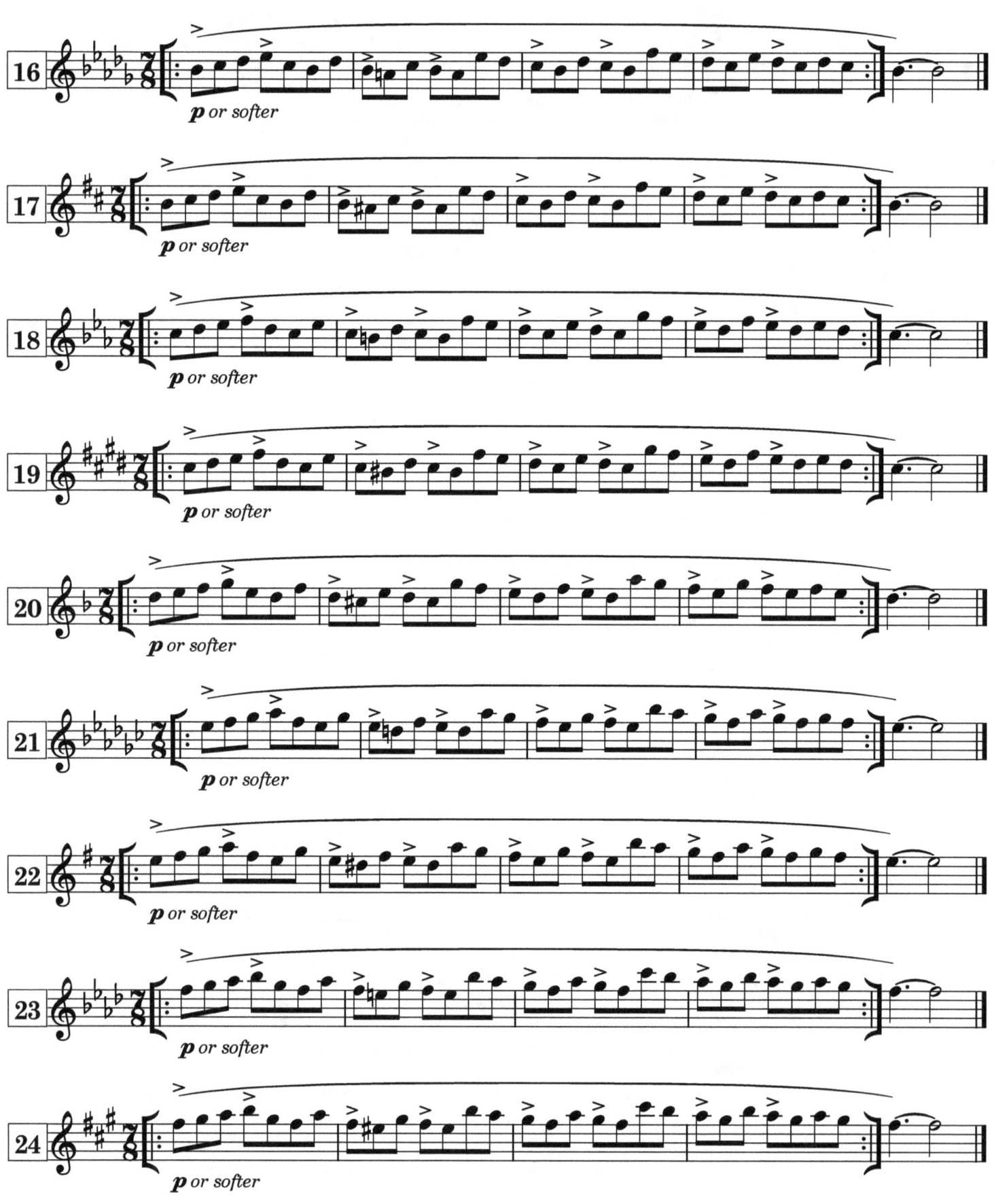

Study 7C - Wholetone

TTS-7C
Bryan Davis

> Given how mouthpiece-obsessed we brass players tend to be, I'm not sure if Study 3C or 7C should be our favourite!
>
> All the wholetone exercises in this book are notated without key signature, so please make sure to follow the accidentals carefully. The physical approach remains the same. Take a deep breath and engage your breath support. We're aiming to play as softly and smoothly as possible. Practice slowly to begin with, slurring to keep the airflow smooth. When the sequence of notes becomes more familiar, then alternate repeats slurred and tongued.

©2020, Airflow Music

airflowmusic.com

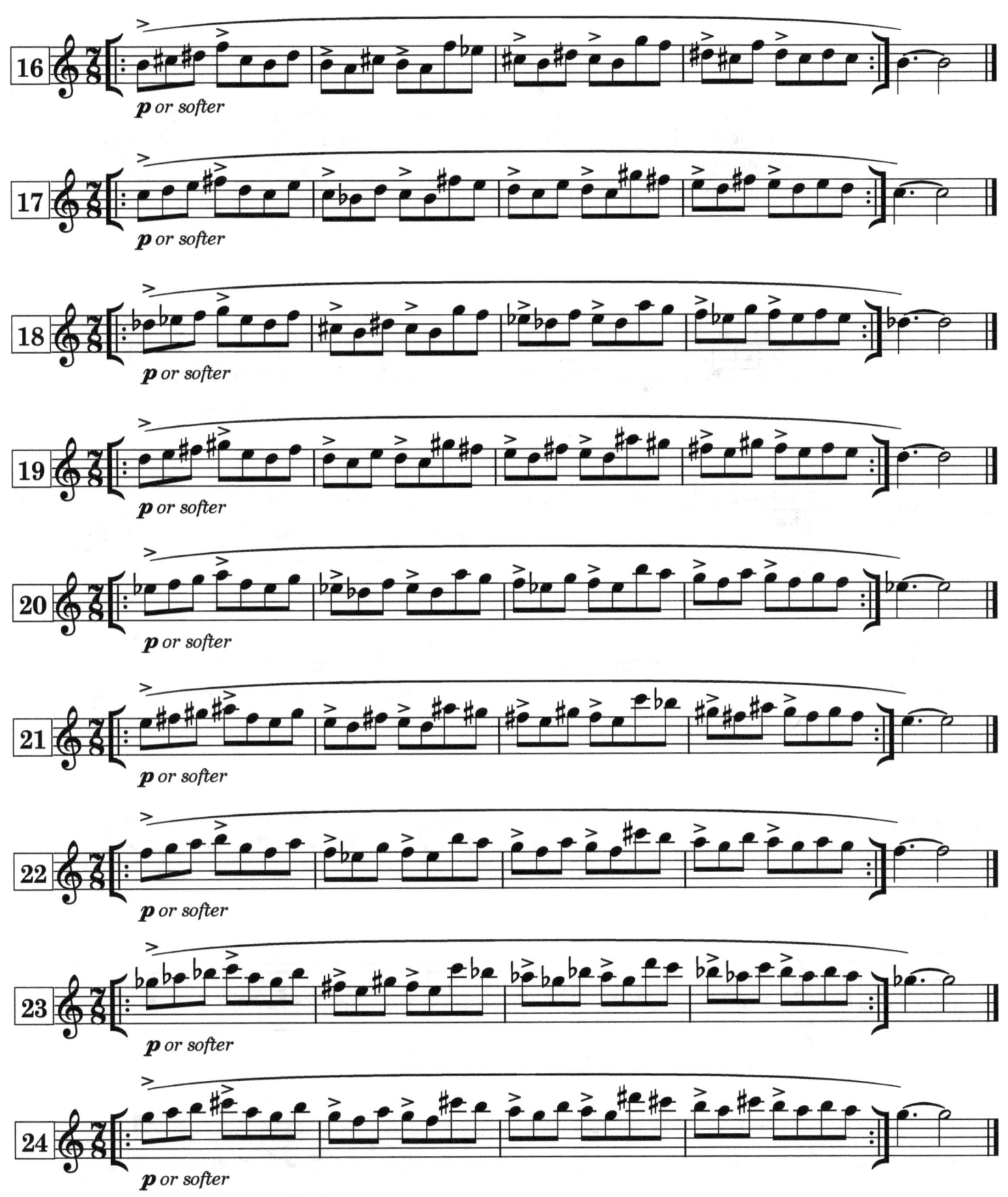

Study 7D - Diminished

TTS-7D
Bryan Davis

The Diminished scale exercises are notated in open key, so please read the accidentals carefully. Practice softly and slowly to begin with, focusing on trying to get from one note to the next as smoothly and beautifully as possible, whether slurring or tonguing. Don't forget to mark the accented notes by tapping your foot and applying a breath accent. Repeat each line as many times as possible in one breath.

airflowmusic.com ©2020, Airflow Music

TTS-7D

Study 8A - Major

TTS-8A   Bryan Davis

> In Studies 5 and 8, in this book, there is a particular pitfall to watch out for. Namely, be careful with the large interval drops in the 2nd and 3rd bars - in the case of the Major and Minor key versions, this is the perfect 5th between the 3rd and 4th beat of the bar. I recommend that you resist the temptation to drop your jaw when playing these larger intervals. Doing so is an unnecessary habit developed by many players, which affects ones ability to play fluidly across the entire range of the instrument. To avoid it, practice slowly through that section, and concentrate on maintaining the same level of mouthpiece pressure for both notes. The interval will most likely feel a little compressed and uncertain at first but, with repetition, the tongue arch will become accustomed to lowering sufficiently without the jaw movement.

©2020, Airflow Music   airflowmusic.com

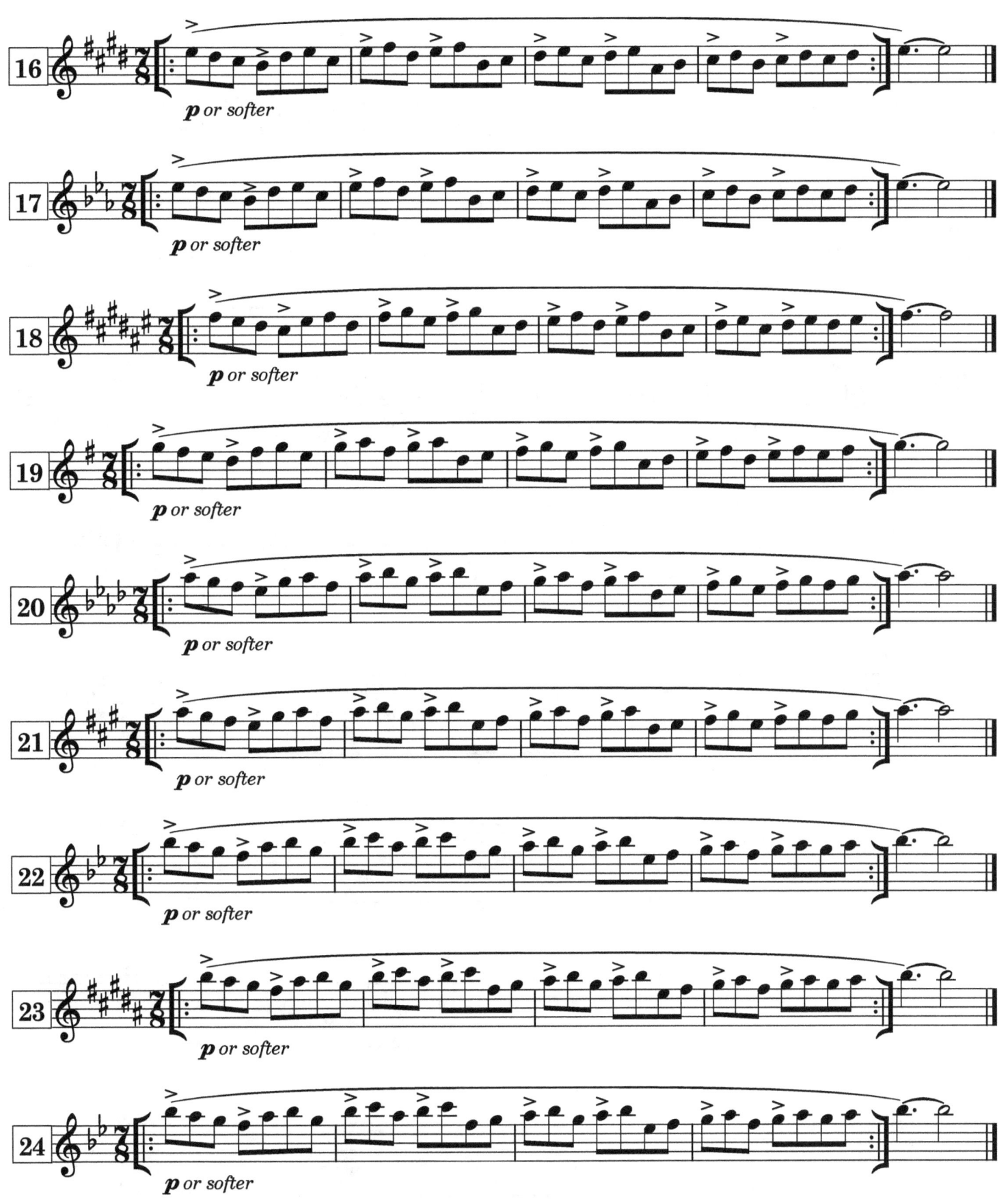

Study 8B - Harmonic Minor

TTS-8B

Bryan Davis

> The principal goal of these exercises is to play as softly, smoothly and effortlessly as possible. Mark time by tapping your foot on each accented note, and applying a breath accent. Please remember that the beaming/accent pattern has changed for Studies 5-8.
>
> Pay careful attention, once again, to the large interval drops in the 2nd and 3rd bars of this Study. Learning to execute these without dropping your jaw will be hugely beneficial for your overall playing. Study 8B is based on the Harmonic Minor scale, so these exercises flow slightly differently to 8A. Observe the key signature and accidentals carefully.

airflowmusic.com

©2020, Airflow Music

TTS-8B

93

Study 8C – Wholetone

TTS-8C
Bryan Davis

All the Wholetone Scale Studies in this book are notated in open key, so please read the accidentals carefully. Studies 5C and 8C contain the widest interval drops in this entire collection – the minor 6th drop in the 2nd and 3rd bars of each line – so they should be approached carefully, as I have detailed elsewhere. Practice slowly and concentrate on maintaining the same mouthpiece pressure for both notes in the interval. Doing so will help you maintain the same jaw position, and only alter the tongue arch position for each note. The lower note of the interval may seem unsteady at first, but this will improve with practice.

©2020, Airflow Music

airflowmusic.com

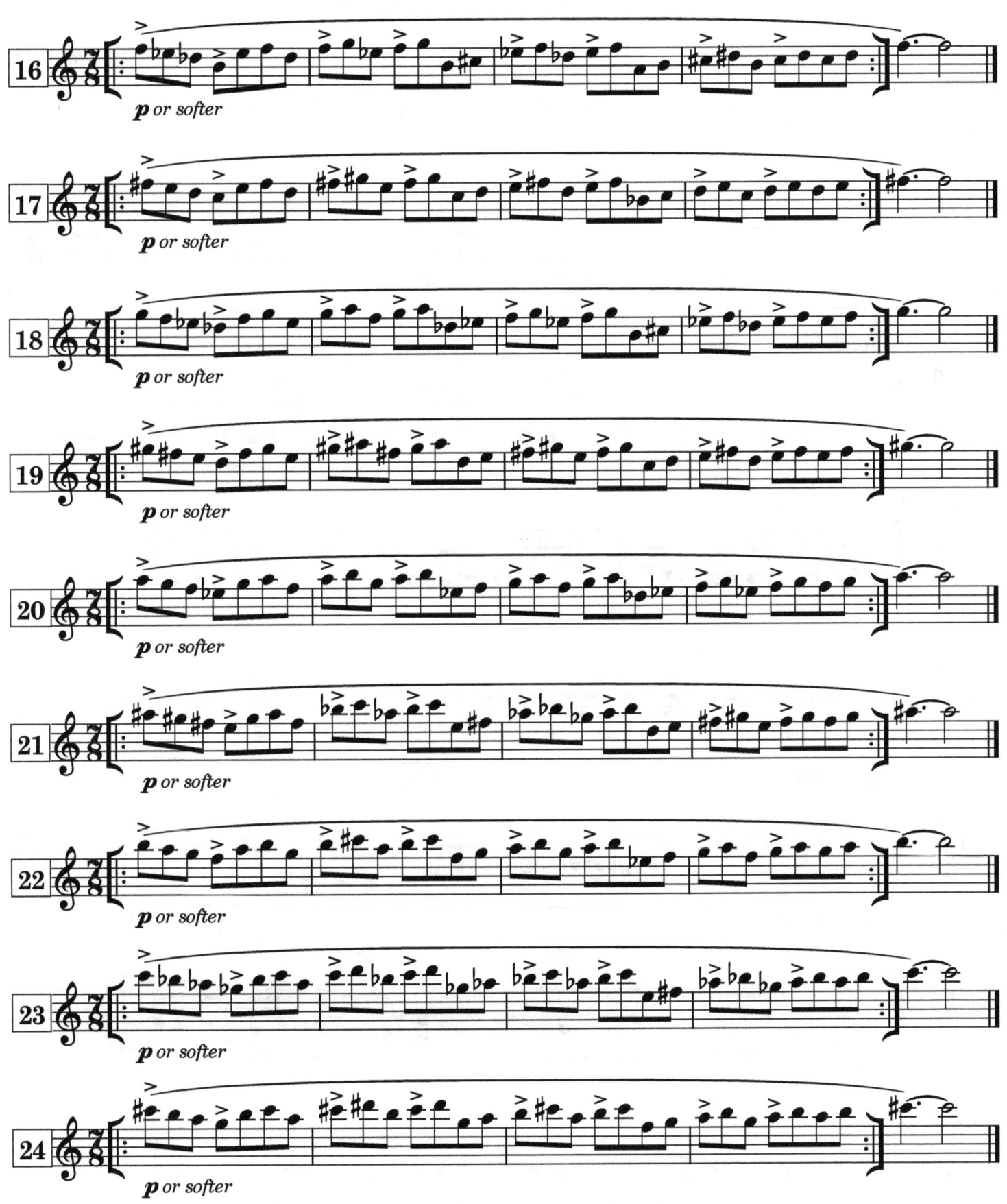

Study 8D – Diminished

TTS-8D

Bryan Davis

You have reached the final study in this book! Well done, and I hope you've had fun practicing all the studies up to this point. Read on and then go practice!

Once again, the Diminished Scale studies are all notated in open key, so please read the accidentals carefully. The overall approach is the same for all of these studies - we are aiming to play as softly. smoothly and evenly as possible. Play each line as many times as possible in one breath. Mark the accented notes with a breath accent and by tapping your foot. Practiced slurred to begin with, then alternate repeats slurred and tongued, once you are familiar with the pattern. Start out as slowly as necessary and gradually work up to the target tempo.

www.ingramcontent.com/pod-product-compliance
Lightning Source LLC
Chambersburg PA
CBHW080415170426
43194CB00015B/2818